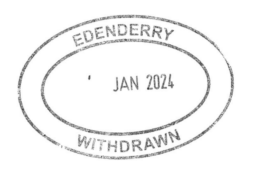

EDENDERRY

JAN 2024

WITHDRAWN

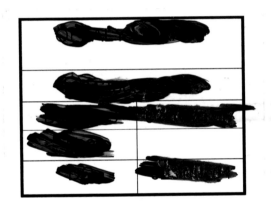

A+ books

Animal Kingdom

MAMMALS

by Lisa J. Amstutz

Consultant: Jackie Gai, DVM
Wildlife Veterinarian

raintree
a Capstone company — publishers for children

Raintree is an imprint of Capstone Global Library Limited, a company incorporated in England and Wales having its registered office at 264 Banbury Road, Oxford, OX2 7DY – Registered company number: 6695582

www.raintree.co.uk
myorders@raintree.co.uk

Text © Capstone Global Library Limited 2017
The moral rights of the proprietor have been asserted.

All rights reserved. No part of this publication may be reproduced in any form or by any means (including photocopying or storing it in any medium by electronic means and whether or not transiently or incidentally to some other use of this publication) without the written permission of the copyright owner, except in accordance with the provisions of the Copyright, Designs and Patents Act 1988 or under the terms of a licence issued by the Copyright Licensing Agency, Saffron House, 6–10 Kirby Street, London EC1N 8TS (www.cla.co.uk). Applications for the copyright owner's written permission should be addressed to the publisher.

Edited by Kathryn Clay
Designed by Rick Korab and Juliette Peters
Picture research by Kelly Garvin
Production by Gene Bentdahl
Originated by Capstone Global Library LTD
Printed and bound in China.

ISBN 978 1 4747 3463 9
21 20 19 18 17
10 9 8 7 6 5 4 3 2 1

British Library Cataloguing in Publication Data
A full catalogue record for this book is available from the British Library.

Acknowledgements
We would like to thank the following for permission to reproduce photographs: Alamy/Nigel Dennis/imageBROKER, 25 (b); Getty Images/Merlin D Tutle, 30 (bl); Minden Pictures: Flip Nicklin, 30 (tl), Michael Durham, 20 (br), Peter Verhoog/Buiten-beeld, 11 (t), Will-Burrard Lucas/NPL, 26 (t), Yva Momatiuk and John Eastcott, 29 (tr); Shutterstock: 06photo, 20-21, 1000 Words, 13 (tr), A_lein, 24 (m), A Periam Photography, 17 (bl), Abeselom Zerit, 7 (r), Agustin Esmoris, 25 (t), andamanec, 14 (tm), Andywak, 30 (br), anshu18, cover (bl), Anton_Ivanov, 18 (m), AuntSpray, 29 (br), Baronb, 22 (t), BarryTuck, 29 (tl), Bartosz Budrewicz, 20 (t), Ben Queenborough, 18 (bm), BGSmith, 12 (br), bikeriderlondon, 10-11, Bildagentur Zoonar GmbH, 12 (bl), Chad Wright Photographt, 12, (tr), chloe7992, 20 (ml), Christian Musat, 16 (b), Christopher Medar, 31 (tr), City Escapes Nature Photo, 12 (tl), costas anton dumitrescu, 27 (m), Cylonphoto, 23 (b), Dan Holm, 31 (bl), David Steele, 10 (bl), djgis, cover, 1 (bkg), Dmitri Gomon, 6 (l), Edwin Butter, 26 (tm), Efimova Anna, 24-25, Eric Isselee, cover, (tr), Ermolaev Alexander, 23 (t), Felix Mizioznikov, 19 (mr), fish 1715, 28 (bl), FloriaStock, 28 (t), fotofactory, 19 (ml), Four Oaks, 5 (b), francesco de marco, 5 (t), 22 (br), George Lamson, 8 (t), Greg Amptman cover (br), GUDKOV ANDREY, back cover, cover (tl), 24 (b), horseman, 26 (b), Hung Chung Chih, 22 (bl), idiz, 7 (bl), Igor Chernomorchenck, 1 (tr), jo Crebbin, 19 (t), Johan Swanepoel, 20 (mr), Johnny Adolphson, 1 (br), JOHNTHAN PLEDGER, 24 (t), Joost van Uffelen, 6-7, 19 (b), Joseph Sohm, 28 (m), kesipun, 4-5, Kristian Bell, 6 (r), kungverylucky, 1 (l), Lamberrto, 8-9, leungchopan, 13 (tl), lightpoet, 11 (m), Longjourneys, 18-19, Lovely Bird, 27 (b), Luiz Kagiyama, 31 (br), marekuliasz, 15 (b), Mari Swanepoel, 30 (tr), Mariska Vermji-van Dijk, 21 (m), MartinMaritz, 10 (tr), Menno Schaefer, 7 (t), Modens Trolle, 13 (b), MyImages-Micha, 10 (br), nattanan726, 21 (tl), Nattle, 2-3, nialat, 17 (tl), outdoorsman, 10 (tl), Peter Schwarz, 9 (t), PHOTOCREO Michal Bednarek, 32, Prazis, 14-15, Rachele Totaro IT, 22-23, ranchorunner, 20 (bl), Raymond Llewellyn, 17 (br), reptiles4all, 21 (b), Robin D. Williams, 15 (t), Ramon Carretero, 14 (bm), Rich Carey, 28 (br), Sergey Krasnoshchokov, 26 (bm), smereka, 22 (m), Stacey Ann Alberts, 16-17, Stephane Bidouze, 14 (t), Stephen Coburn, 8 (b), Stuart G. Porter, 21 (tr), 31 (tl), Tatiana Grozetskaya, 28-29, Tony Baggett, 29 (bl), Tony Campbell, 14 (b), Tony Rix, 27 (t), Tory Kallman, 4 (inset), Vladimir Cech Jr, 12-13, Vladmir Melnik, 18 (b), Volodymyr Goinyk, 17 (tr), Welson Schioneger, 11 (b), worldwildlifewonders, 18 (t), zahorec, 26-27, Zuzule, 9 (b)

Artistic elements: Shutterstock: abracadabra, De-V, Hein Nattle, Nouwens, yyang, Zhenyakot

Every effort has been made to contact copyright holders of material reproduced in this book. Any omissions will be rectified in subsequent printings if notice is given to the publisher.

All the internet addresses (URLs) given in this book were valid at the time of going to press. However, due to the dynamic nature of the internet, some addresses may have changed, or sites may have changed or ceased to exist since publication. While the author and publisher regret any inconvenience this may cause readers, no responsibility for any such changes can be accepted by either the author or the publisher.

CONTENTS

What are mammals?

Mammals are a group of animals that have hair or fur. Most have live young. They drink milk from their mothers after they're born. Elephants, bats and dolphins are mammals. And so are you!

class
a smaller group of living things; mammals are in the class Mammalia

kingdom
one of five very large groups into which all living things are placed; the two main kingdoms are plants and animals; mammals belong to the animal kingdom

phylum
(FIE-lum)
a group of living things with a similar body plan; mammals belong to the phylum Chordata (kawr-DEY-tuh); reptiles, fish, amphibians and birds are also in this group

vertebrate
(VUR-tuh-brut)
an animal that has a backbone; mammals are vertebrates

species

(SPEE-sees)
a group of animals
that are alike and can
produce young with each
other; there are more
than 5,000 species
of mammals

warm-blooded

having a body
temperature that
stays about the same all
the time, no matter the
surroundings; mammals
and birds are
warm-blooded

order

a group of
living things that is
smaller than a class;
there are more
than 20 orders
of mammals

live young

babies born directly
from their mother,
rather than from laid
eggs; nearly all mammals
give birth to live young;
only two mammals
lay eggs

Getting into groups

cetaceans
(si-TEY-shunz)
mammals that live
in the ocean; whales
and dolphins
are cetaceans

**hoofed
mammals**
also called ungulates
(UN-guh-lits); animals
with a hard covering
on each toe; horses,
giraffes and goats are
hoofed mammals

monotremes
(MON-uh-treemz)
mammals that lay
eggs and have no
nipples; echidnas
(ih-KID-nuhz) are
monotremes

goat

rodents
small mammals whose teeth never stop growing and must be regularly worn down by chewing; squirrels and mice are rodents

placental
(pluh-SEN-tuhl)
mammals that carry their young inside their bodies; the young are born alive; humans are placental

squirrel

marsupials
(mar-SOO-pee-uhlz)
mammals that carry their young in a pouch; kangaroos are marsupials

primates
mammals with five fingers, five toes and forward-facing eyes; monkeys are primates

Circle of life

sea lion pup

life cycle
the series of changes that take place in a living thing, from birth to death

mate
to join together to make young

pup
a young dog, rat, seal or sea lion

juvenile
(JOO-vuh-nile): a young animal that is not fully grown

nurse
to drink mother's milk; baby mammals nurse from their mothers

wean
to stop needing mother's milk; weaned animals replace the milk with solid food

lion cubs

cub
a young lion or bear

foal
a young horse

adult
a fully grown animal

Home, sweet home

Mammals live almost everywhere, from hot deserts to the icy tundra. They are found on every continent and in every ocean.

habitat
the type of place and conditions in which a plant or animal lives

arctic fox

tundra
(TUN-druh): a large, flat area of land found in the Arctic; no trees grow in the tundra, and the ground is always frozen; moose and arctic foxes live in the tundra

hippo

freshwater
water that does not contain salt; most ponds, rivers, lakes and streams are freshwater bodies; hippos and beavers live in freshwater areas

desert
(DEH-zuhrt): a dry area that gets little rain; camels live in deserts

howler monkey

rainforest
a thick area of trees where rain falls almost every day; sloths and howler monkeys live in rainforests

porpoise

ocean

a large body of salt water;
whales, dolphins and
porpoises live in oceans

forest

an area with many trees; deer
and wolves live in forests

bison

plain

a large, flat area of land
with few trees; bison and
pronghorn antelope live
on the plains

What's for dinner?

Mammals eat just about anything, from tiny insects to tall giraffes. Some mammals eat only plants. Others eat a mix of plants and animals.

hyena

scavenger
(SKAV-in-jer)
an animal that feeds on animals that are already dead; wild African dogs and hyenas are scavengers

carnivore
(KAHR-nuh-vor)
an animal that eats only meat; large cats, wolves and sea lions are carnivores

sea lion

insectivore
(in-SEK-tuh-vor)
a mammal that eats insects; moles and hedgehogs are insectivores

mole

omnivore
(OM-nuh-vor)
an animal that eats both plants and animals; black bears eat berries, grasses, fish and small mammals

herbivore
(HUR-buh-vor)
an animal that eats
only plants; giant
pandas eat 9 to 18
kilograms (20 to 40
pounds) of bamboo
each day

sheep

graze
to eat grass
and other plants
growing in a field;
cows and sheep
graze

predator
(PRED-uh-tur)
an animal that
hunts other animals
for food; all big cats
are predators

**food
chain**
a series of living
things in which
each one eats the
one before it

prey
(PRAY)
an animal hunted
by another animal
for food; zebras
are often prey
for lions

Sensing the world

Is this something to eat?
Is danger nearby?
Mammals use their senses to explore the world.

echo
(EK-oh): the sound that returns after a travelling sound hits an object; bats use echoes to find their way in the dark

hearing
for many mammals, such as foxes, hearing is their strongest sense

sight
many mammals have good eyesight; lions have special eyes that help them see in the dark

whisker
a long, stiff hair growing on the faces and bodies of some animals; a fox's whiskers can help it hunt or find its way in the dark

scent trail
a smell left behind by an animal; some mammals follow scent trails

musk
a strong smell made by some mammals

smell
mammals often use their noses to find food and mates

urine
an animal's liquid body waste; urine is used as a signal to other animals

scat
an animal's solid body waste; scat can also be a signal to other animals

Hot or not?

Mammals have many adaptations for keeping their temperature just right.

adaptation
(a-dap-TAY-shuhn)
a change a living thing goes through over time to better fit in with its surroundings

shiver
to shake or tremble with cold; shivering keeps warm-blooded animals from getting too cold

hibernate

(HYE-bur-nate): to spend the winter months in a deep sleep; black bears can go for more than seven months without eating

nocturnal

(nok-TUR-nuhl): active at night; coyotes escape the desert heat by resting during the day and hunting at night

seal

underfur

a fine, soft layer of fur under the outer fur; seals and beavers have underfur

blubber

a thick layer of fat under the skin of marine mammals that helps to keep them warm

sweat

to give off wetness through small holes in the skin; sweating helps horses cool down

Splish splash!

Some mammals spend most or all of their time in the water. They come to the surface for air.

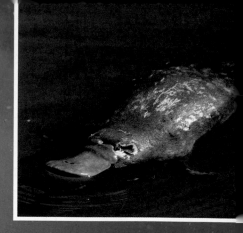

blowhole
a hole on the top of a whale's head; whales breathe air through blowholes

sea lion
a noisy sea mammal with long flippers and small ear flaps

walrus
a large sea mammal that has flippers, large tusks and wrinkled skin

platypus

an Australian mammal with webbed feet; the platypus is one of the few mammals that lays eggs

baleen

long, fringed plates in the mouths of some whales; the baleen takes in food and pushes out water

beaver

an animal with a wide, flat tail; beavers build dams across streams

sea lion

flipper

one of the broad, flat limbs of a sea creature; flippers help seals and sea lions to swim

fin

a body part that some sea mammals use to swim and steer in water

tail

the part at the back end of an animal's body; sea mammals use their tails to push them through the water

Heat seekers

Some mammals like it hot! They make their homes in hot, dry desert areas.

lion
the second-largest member of the cat family, after tigers

javelina
(ha-vuh-LEEN-uh)
also called a peccary; javelinas have tough mouths that allow them to eat cacti

jackal
a medium-sized member of the dog family

jackrabbit
a hare with long legs and ears

kangaroo rat
a small rodent with large back legs and feet; kangaroo rats get the water they need from the seeds they eat

fennec fox

weighs only 0.9 to 1.4 kilograms (2 to 3 pounds); this African fox uses its large ears to shed heat and stay cool

gazelle

(guh-ZEL): a small antelope; gazelles run very fast

cheetah

a large spotted member of the cat family; cheetahs are the fastest land mammal

camel

an animal with one or two humps to store fat and water; thick eyelashes keep sand out of their eyes

jerboa

a hopping desert rodent with large ears, long back legs and a long tail

Pets and more

Mammals help humans in many ways. Some make good pets. Others give us food or clothing.

livestock
animals that are kept on a farm; sheep are livestock

dairy
(DAIR-ee)
having to do with milk products; dairy farmers raise cows for their milk

draught animal
an animal used for pulling heavy loads; oxen are often used as draught animals

wool
the soft, thick, curly hair of sheep or goats; wool is used to make yarn and fabric

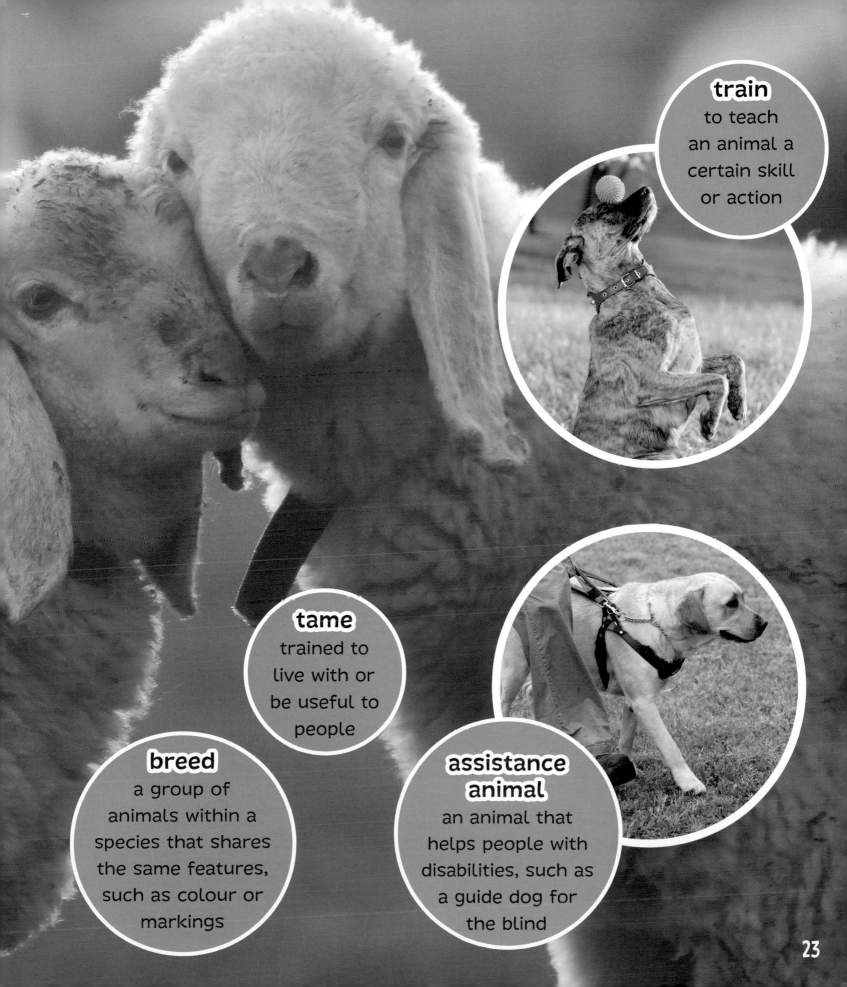

train
to teach an animal a certain skill or action

tame
trained to live with or be useful to people

breed
a group of animals within a species that shares the same features, such as colour or markings

assistance animal
an animal that helps people with disabilities, such as a guide dog for the blind

23

The hunt is on

Some mammals are hunters. Others are hunted. Mammals have many ways to stay safe from predators.

scent
the smell of something; skunks use a strong scent to scare away predators

warning colours
markings on an animal, like a skunk's stripes, that tell predators to stay away

horn
a hard, bony growth on the head of some animals; rhinos use their horn to fight off predators

camouflage
(KA-muh-flahzh): colouring that makes animals look like their surroundings; a leopard's spotted coat helps it to blend in with forest shadows

spine
a sharp, pointed growth; porcupines are covered with spines for protection

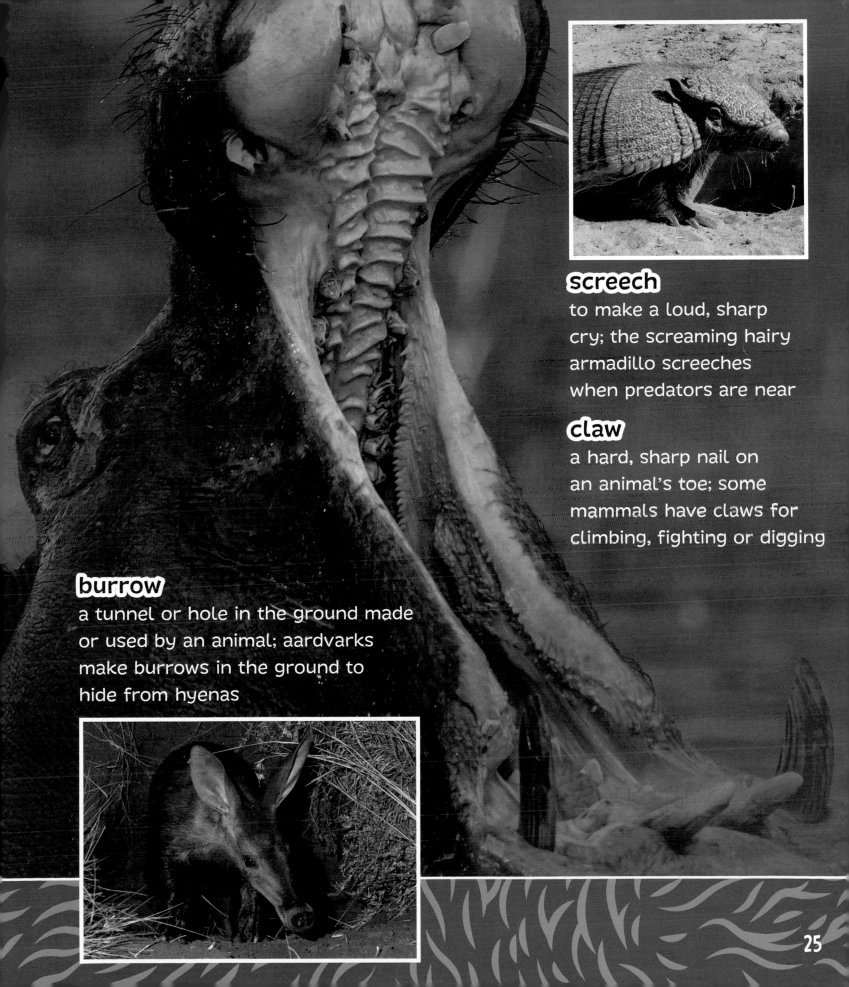

screech

to make a loud, sharp
cry; the screaming hairy
armadillo screeches
when predators are near

claw

a hard, sharp nail on
an animal's toe; some
mammals have claws for
climbing, fighting or digging

burrow

a tunnel or hole in the ground made
or used by an animal; aardvarks
make burrows in the ground to
hide from hyenas

On the move

Humans get most places by walking. But some mammals can fly, swim or hop. They have many ways of getting around.

glide
to move smoothly; flying squirrels glide through the air by spreading out folds of skin on the sides of their bodies

grasp
to grab and hold firmly; monkeys use their hands, feet and prehensile (pri-HEN-sil) tails to move through the trees

snowshoe
to walk on snow using special frames (snowshoes) strapped to a person's feet; the wide hooves of caribou act like snowshoes

gallop
to run fast; a horse gallops by lifting all four of its hooves off the ground as it runs

pounce
to jump or swoop suddenly to catch prey; mountain lions and other big cats pounce

migrate
(MYE-grate): to move from one place to another when seasons change in order to find food or to mate; elephants migrate

fly
to travel through the air; bats are the only mammals that can fly

Mammals in danger

Some human actions can be harmful to animals. Laws can protect animals and their homes.

preserve
(pri-ZURV)
a place where animals can live and be protected from hunters

climate change
changes in weather patterns caused by human activities; these changes can harm animals

water pollution
harmful materials that damage the water and hurt the animals that live in it

habitat loss
loss of animal homes, usually due to human activities such as logging or building

oil spill
the release of oil into the water from a ship or pipeline; oil spills can be deadly to sea mammals

poacher
(POH-cher)
a person who collects or kills animals illegally; in South Africa rhinos are caught and sold by poachers

fishing nets
seals can get tangled in fishing nets

logging
the cutting down of trees; logging in the rainforest causes animals to lose their homes

extinct
(ek-STINGKT)
no longer living; an extinct animal is one that has died out, with no more of its kind on Earth; woolly mammoths have been extinct for 4,000 years

endangered
in danger of dying out

Fun facts

Blue whales are Earth's largest animals. They can reach 30 metres (100 feet) in length and weigh up to 181 metric tons (200 tons).

A **newborn elephant** weighs about 91 kilograms (200 pounds).

The smallest mammal is the **Kitti's hognosed bat**. At just 2 grams (0.07 ounces), it is the size of a bumblebee.

Koalas sleep 16 to 18 hours each day.

Cheetahs can run up to 113 kilometres (70 miles) per hour.

A **newborn kangaroo** is smaller than a cherry. When it grows up, it will be as tall as an adult human.

A **giraffe's** tongue is 46 to 51 centimetres (18 to 20 inches) long. The long tongue can wrap around branches and tear off leaves from tall trees.

anteater

Anteaters, pangolins and many whales don't have teeth.

FIND OUT MORE

Mammals (Focus On: Classification), Stephen Savage (Wayland, 2014)

Marvellous Mammals (Extreme Animals), Isabel Thomas (Raintree, 2012)

Why Do Mammals Have Fur? (Wildlife Wonders), Pat Jacobs (Franklin Watts, 2014)

WEBSITES

animals.howstuffworks.com/mammals
Visit this website to read articles about different kinds of mammals.

animals.nationalgeographic.com/animals/ mammals
Pictures, videos and information about mammals.